Working Together

Program Authors

Connie Juel, Ph.D.

Jeanne R. Paratore, Ed.D.

Deborah Simmons, Ph.D.

Sharon Vaughn, Ph.D.

ISBN 0-328-21457-4
Copyright © 2008 Pearson Education, Inc.

7 8 9 10 V011 12 11 10 09 08 07
CC1

Editorial Offices: Glenview, Illinois • Parsippany, New Jersey • New York, New York
Sales Offices: Boston, Massachusetts • Duluth, Georgia • Glenview, Illinois
Coppell, Texas • Sacramento, California • Mesa, Arizona

PEARSON
Scott
Foresman

UNIT 2 Contents

Working Together

DANGER! 4

What can we do in a dangerous situation?

Team Spirit 26

What makes a team?

Sharing 48

When does sharing make sense?

Side by Side 72

When should we work together?
When should we work alone?

LET'S CELEBRATE 100

How can we contribute to a celebration?

Contents

DANGER!

Let's Find Out

6 Danger!
When must you check for danger?

12 Danger on the Job
Some jobs have danger.

16 Fire on the Hill
A family gets away.

24 Fire Safety at Home
Do you have a plan?

See page 25 for My New Words!

Chad and Mitch hunt for a spot to swim. Can they swim in this pond?

Stop! Much danger is in this pond. It is not a good pond to swim in. Chad and Mitch must hunt around for a spot to swim.

Whit hunts for a snack. She must check for danger. Can Whit munch this? Can Whit munch that? Stop! Nothing is fit to munch.

Whit must ask Mom. Mom has enough snacks that Whit can munch. Mom will fetch a snack that Whit can munch. Whit will munch and munch. Yum, yum!

Look at all eight. When must you check them? They tell that there is danger. Which tells not to set fire at camp?

When you swim, stop and think. Check it! Is it a fit spot to swim?

When you munch, stop and think. Check it! Is it fit to munch?

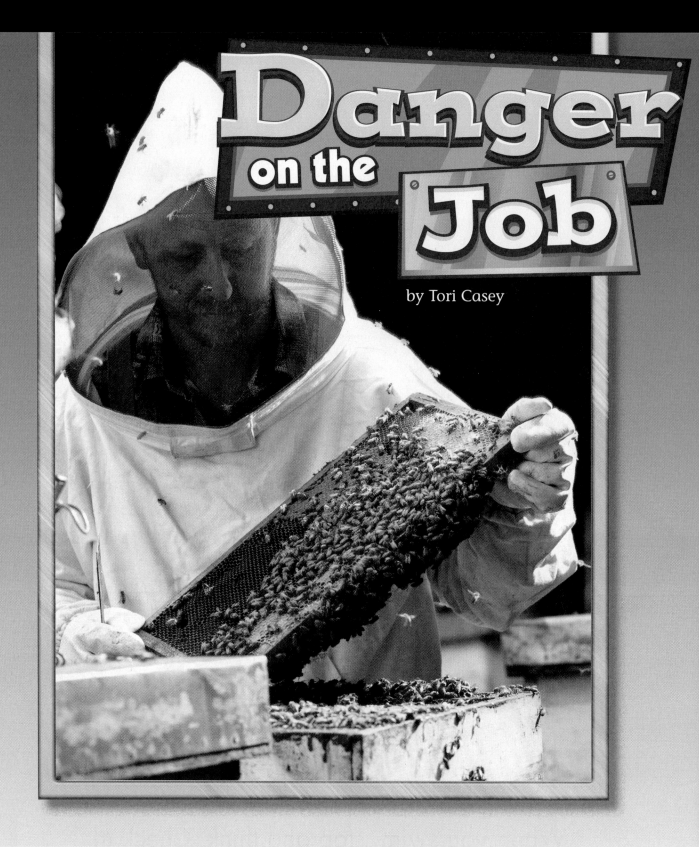

Danger
on the Job

by Tori Casey

Which jobs have danger? Ben has danger on his job. Bugs are buzzing around. Buzzing bugs can sting. Check what Ben has on. Is it helping enough?

Jen is fixing a big crack. Jen has a drill.
Is drilling a danger? Check what Jen has on. Is
it helping?

Gus is standing up on top. Gus is not resting. Gus has a big branch to cut. Then he must cut eight others. Check what Gus has on. What is helping him?

Lots of kids are crossing. Tiff is helping them. Nothing will hit them. What is helping us see them?

FIRE
on the Hill

by Linda Miller   illustrated by Adam Gustavson

Chuck lives with his mom and dad next to this hill. Chuck has lots of pals on this hill. It is such a grand spot.

Look! Chuck spots fire. Lots are working to stop it. Lots are helping, but they can not act fast enough. It is hot, and nothing can stop it.

Chuck is thinking, "I wish I could help them."
But men in trucks are yelling at him, "You must
run! There is much danger! You must get away fast!"

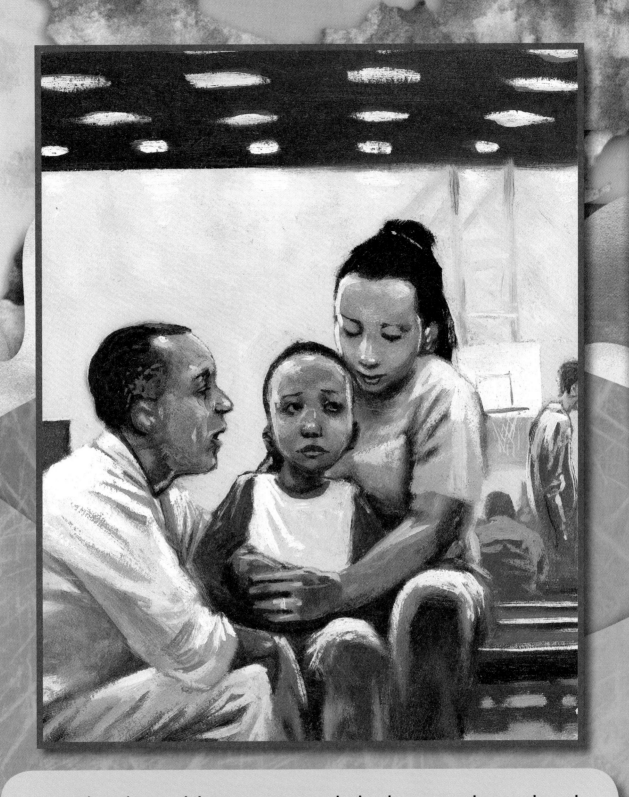

Chuck and his mom and dad run to his school.
Chuck is sad. His mom and dad hug him.
Chuck is resting and thinking.

Chuck spots a bunch of his pals.
Around eight they get good news. The danger
is ending. They can go back.

Chuck and his dad are thanking the men for helping them.

Chuck spots a big black patch on his hill. But the fire is not there. The hill will be green soon.

Chuck is glad. Chuck is thinking that his hill is such a grand spot.

Fire Safety
at Home

- Make sure you have smoke alarms in your home.

- Make a fire escape plan with your family. Practice your escape plan at least twice a year.

- In case of a fire, get out of your home. Once you are out, stay out!

- Call 9-1-1 from a neighbor's home.

24

My New Words

around*   The new kids walk **around** school. The top spins **around.**

danger   **Danger** is when someone or something can be hurt.

drill   When you **drill,** you make a hole in something.

eight*   The number between seven and nine is **eight**.

enough*   We have **enough** snacks for all.

nothing*   There is **nothing** in the empty closet.

patch   A **patch** is a piece of ground. A **patch** is also something used to fix a hole or a tear.

*tested high-frequency words

Contents

Team Spirit

Let's Find Out

28 Team Spirit
Teams can be fun.

32 The Red Fins
The Red Fins swim like fish!

36 Jon and Jen
Jon and Jen have team spirit.

46 Be a Good Sport!
What is a good sport?

See page 47 for My New Words!

Team Spirit

Teams have fun. It is fun if you can win. It is fun if you can not win. It is fun just to get together with pals.

How did this team win? Kids helped hit. Kids helped catch. Kids helped run fast. Kids helped win.

This team dug and planted. Can one
kid carry this big pot? One kid can not. It is
too heavy. Can the kids lift it together? Yes.
They lifted it. This plant will get big with sun
and water.

This swing is for kids. Kids helped build it.
It was a big job. This team worked and worked.
Now kids can run and jump and have fun.

The Red Fins

by Megan Brooks

The Red Fins is a swimming team. Swimming is fun. But swimming is not just getting wet. The Red Fins must work. The Red Fins can build a winning team.

Some Red Fins jumped in the water. The rest were sitting and clapping. They yelled, "Swim fast, Red Fins! Swim fast!"

Then Beth stepped up. Red Fins stopped clapping and sat still. Beth jumped and slipped into the water. Splash!

Yes. Beth was swimming her best! The Red Fins clapped. Will Beth win? Will the Red Fins win?

When it ended, the Red Fins got this. It is not heavy. Beth can carry it.

This was fun. The Red Fins patted backs and grinned. The Red Fins still must work. The Red Fins will build a winning team.

Jon and Jen

by Laura Edwards
illustrated by Barbara Fiore

Jon and Jen were best pals. They batted on the Cubs team.

Jon batted well. His batting was tops. Smack! Jon hit it!

"Go, Jon!" yelled Jen.
Jen batted next. Jen swung and missed.
Swing! Swing! Swing! Jen did not hit.

Jen wished she batted well.

"I wish I batted like you," Jen told Jon. "You bat the best!"

Jon said, "I will help with this. Look!" Jon swung and hit. Swing! Smack!

Jen saw how Jon hit. Jen swung and hit.
Swing! Smack!
"Top job!" grinned Jon. Jen felt glad.

Jon and Jen were on the Jets team too. Jon and Jen ran on this team.

Jen ran well. Her running was tops. Swish! Jen ran fast.

"Go, Jen!" yelled Jon.

Jon ran next. Jon ran and ran. But Jon did not run fast. Kids ran past Jon.

Jon wished he ran fast.

"I wish I ran like you," Jon told Jen. "You run the best!"

Jen said, "I will help with this. Look!" Jen ran. Jen ran fast.

Jon saw how Jen ran. Jon ran. Jon ran fast.
"Top job!" grinned Jen. "You ran fast!" Jon
felt glad.

Jen helped Jon carry heavy water jugs. Then Jen and Jon sipped water and chatted.

"We will build top teams together!" grinned Jen and Jon.

Be a Good Sport!

I'm a good sport. I come to practice on time.

I follow the rules of the game.

I always play fair.

I give high fives to kids on the other team after the game.

46

My New Words

build*   To **build** is to make something by putting things together.

carry*   When you **carry** something, you take it from one place to another.

heavy*   If something is **heavy**, it is hard to lift or carry. It weighs a lot.

team   A **team** is a group of people working or playing together.

water*   **Water** is liquid that fills oceans, rivers, lakes, and ponds. **Water** falls from the sky as rain.

*tested high-frequency words

Contents

Sharing

50

Let's Find Out

Sharing

Kids share in many ways.

58

Who Can Share a Tree?

A tree has a lot to give.

64

A Snack for Grace

Grace shares too much.

70

Share with a Brother

What can a brother share?

See page 71 for My New Words!

Sharing

Kids can enjoy lakes. It is fun to swim. Splash! Splash!

Kids can wade. Kids can jump from wave to wave. It makes them laugh.

It is such fun to share the lake!

Kids can bake. It is fun helping Mom. Kids can bake cakes. Kids can enjoy a few cakes. Yum, yum! Save a plate of cake for Dad!

It is such fun to share cake!

Kids can enjoy games. Take a bag. Toss
it toward a spot. If it lands in the spot, make
another toss. Thud! Thud!

It is such fun to share games!

This is a bunk bed. It has two beds in it. Kids can share it. Kids can sit on it. Kids can rest on it. Kids can go up, up, up to the top!

It is such fun to share a bunk bed!

Who Can Share a Tree?

by Christine Crocker

This nest is made with twigs. The nest sits on a branch in this big tree. The eggs are safe in this place. Who sits on eggs to make them safe?

Look on another branch. This is a web. It looks like lace, but it is a trap. It can catch bugs that run toward it. This is not a safe place for bugs. Run, bugs, run! Run fast!

Take a look at this! Who stops and enjoys a few nuts?

Scratch, scratch! Dig, dig! It will make a space. Plop! It will drop in a nut. It will race to get another. It must hunt and hunt. It must dig and dig. Plop! Plop! It races to get lots of nuts.

61

Nate sits in the shade. Nate rests next to this tree trunk. Nate looks at pages with a grin on his face.

This tree has shade for Nate. It has space for nests made of twigs. It has space for bugs that race and buzz. And it has nuts that drop. This tree shares a lot!

A Snack for Grace

by Linda Cave
illustrated by Michael Rex

Grace gets a big bunch of grapes. Grace gets the grapes wet.

Grace will place the snack on a big plate. Grace will take it out back.

Lin races toward the gate.

"Come in, Lin," yells Grace. "I made a snack. Take a plate."

Yum, yum! Lin will enjoy the grapes.

Dave and Ben race in next.
"Take some grapes," Grace tells them.
Dave and Ben take a plate. It is a good snack.

Lin waves to Sage. Sage runs in.
"Sage, will you sit with us?" asks Grace.
"Take this bunch of grapes."
"Thanks, Grace," Sage tells Grace.

"This plate has just a few grapes left," Sage tells the kids. "Grace gave us lots and lots of grapes. But Grace did not get many grapes."

Just then Rafe races in with another bunch of grapes. Rafe yells, "Look at this snack. It is big. Take some."

"You bet!" the kids tell Rafe. "But Grace gets the best plate!"

Share with a Brother

My New Words

another*   I chose **another** game.

enjoy*   If you **enjoy** something, it makes you happy.

few*   If you have a **few**, you do not have many.

lace   Her dress is made of fancy **lace**.

share   When you **share**, you let someone use something with you.

toward*   He walked **toward** the door.

tree   A **tree** is a large plant with a trunk, branches, and leaves.

*tested high-frequency words

Contents

Side by Side

74

Let's Find Out

Side by Side
Who works together? Who works alone?

80

Animals Together, Animals Alone
Animals work in different ways.

88

Sliding Boxes
Mike has a wise plan.

96

All Work Together
Work together with a giggle and a wiggle!

See page 99 for My New Words!

Side by Side

ants

One ant can not dig this nest. It takes lots and lots of ants instead. This bunch of ants can dig. They make big piles of sand. This will make an ant hill. Ants like to work together.

74

spittlebug

This bug makes an odd nest on thin twigs. It has no help. Look at the nest. It is wet. This bug will hide in its nest. This time one bug can do just fine.

Kids smile while they rake and fill sacks.
Kids like to make big piles. One kid likes to run
across the grass and dive in big piles.

This place will look fine when they are through. Kids like to work together.

The sun has set. The moon shines. Niles sits at his desk and works on his math.

Niles takes his time. Can Niles add nine plus five? Yes!

Niles will not ask for help. This time one kid can do just fine.

Animals Together, Animals Alone

by Jorge Campa

wolves

Who likes to work together? Who does not? This is a pack. This pack looks out for its pups. The pups like chasing other pups for fun.

This pack likes hunting together. When the pack hunts, it has a plan.

Packs like to sing when the moon is shining.

cougar

Look through the grass. This big cat is hiding. But it is not resting. Instead, it is hunting. This big cat does not like hunting with other cats.

It is time to run. This big cat will chase and catch an elk. Run fast, big cat!

penguins

This bunch likes sliding across ice. This bunch likes splashing. This bunch likes diving together and catching fish.

This bunch likes riding on waves for lots and lots of fun. Slide! Splash! Ride!

sloth

This is a sloth. A sloth is not fast. It does not rush. It just hangs from a branch and hides in vines. A sloth is good at taking naps. It is not good at waking up.

A sloth does not spend its time with other sloths. It snacks on buds and twigs. A sloth has an odd life.

SLIDING BOXES

by Elsie Victor

illustrated by R.W. Alley

"This big box has things for sale. Mike, can you lift it?" asked Miss Pine. "Can you take it across to the other side?"

"Yes, I can lift it, and I will take it," grinned Mike. "I like to help."

Miss Pine smiled and rushed off.

Mike lifted and lifted. Mike tugged and tugged. The box slid just an inch on the white tile! Mike was tired.

"This will take some time!" said Mike.

Kate waved to Mike. She wanted to help set up. She grabbed a box with prizes in it.

Kate lifted and lifted. Kate tugged and tugged. Kate was tired.

"This could take till the moon rises! Can I just make this box slide?" Kate asked Mike.

Mike faced Kate.

"I tugged and tugged. This box is not sliding," said Mike. "I will help you with this prize box instead. I have a plan."

Mike placed a line around the box.
"Kate, take this line. Grab an end. We must slide this box," smiled Mike.

Mike tugged the line. Kate tugged the line.
The box was sliding fast. This plan was wise.

"When we are through sliding this box, we
can slide mine," smiled Mike.

"We did it! We make a fine team!"
Mike said.
    "Yes, but now it is time for fun and games!"
said Kate.

All Work Together

by Woody Guthrie

illustrated by Lynne Avril-Cravath

My mommy told me an' the teacher told me, too,
There's all kinds of work that I can do:
Dry my dishes, sweep my floor,
But if we all work together it won't take very long.

We all work together with a wiggle and a giggle,
We all work together with a giggle and a grin.
We all work together with a wiggle and a giggle,
We all work together with a giggle and a grin.

My daddy said,
And my grandpaw, too,
There's work, worka, work
For me to do.
I can paint my fence.
Mow my lawn.
But if we all work together,
Well, it shouldn't take long. So...

We all work together with a wiggle and a giggle,
We all work together with a giggle and a grin.
We all work together with a wiggle and a giggle,
We all work together with a giggle and a grin.
With a wiggle and a giggle and a google and a goggle
And a jigger and a jagger and a giggle and a grin.

My New Words

across*   My friend lives **across** the street.

instead*   **Instead** means in place of something else.

moon*   The **moon** moves around the Earth.

slide   To **slide** is to move in a smooth way. Let's **slide** down the hill.

through*   The kitten ran **through** the house. We learned a new song all the way **through**.

tug   When you **tug**, you pull hard on something.

*tested high-frequency words

Contents

LET'S CELEBRATE

102

Let's Find Out

Let's Celebrate

What do we do for fun times?

110

Big, Big Balloon

Have you ever seen a balloon this big?

116

The Balloon Ride

Meg goes up, up, and away.

124

Make a Greeting Card

Make a card for a friend.

See page 126 for My New Words!
101

LET'S CELEBRATE

Kids can help their mother and father set up for fun times at home. Mom hangs a rope for this game. Dad fills cups with red punch. The kids made a cake.

102

How will they remember this fun time? They will pose and smile!

This bunch of kids will stick pink, white, and red roses in holes. This time the kids will make a throne. Will this big throne be fun? When it is made, the kids will sit on it and ride.

How will they remember this fun time? They will pose and smile!

Kids in this class get set for a fun time. They make a big note. They will poke holes and hang this big note with string.

Miss Grove smiles. "This note is still wet," Miss Grove tells the kids. "You must not touch it yet."

How will they remember this fun time? They will pose and smile!

Hush! Those kids are hiding. They must sit still, as if they froze. They must sit till their pal gets home. Then the kids will jump up. "Surprise!" the kids will yell.

How will they remember this fun time? They will pose and smile!

Big, Big Balloon

by Ed Ward
illustrated by
Gideon Kendall

This man makes big balloons. Today he will plan a new one.

This man's plan looks little. But his balloon's size will be quite big. It will be as big as a big truck. That is a big balloon!

Then the man makes this thing. It is like stone if you touch it. And it is little.

The man looks at this little thing. The man thinks. Is this plan nice? The man will make his balloon just like this little thing, but big.

Next, this man will cut big shapes from thin cloth and put them together. Now this big, big balloon is made.

Then the big balloon is filled with gas. It rises up and up and up. Men's hands grab long ropes. They hope those ropes will not snap. They hope that this balloon's skin has no holes.

It is time for fun. Men's hands grab long
ropes again. They take this big balloon past lots
and lots of shops and people.

Mothers and fathers clap and yell. Kids clap and yell. Kids will remember this big, big balloon!

The Balloon Ride

by Victor Strong
illustrated by Jeff Ebbeler

Rose will be nine. Rose and her pals will have
fun at Rose's home. Meg has a gift for Rose.
"I hope Rose has cake and games," said Meg.

"I will get red and pink and white," said Meg. "I remember that Rose likes those. I will get this balloon too. And this. And this. And this. Then I must rush to Rose's home. I can not miss the fun."

This man has balloons too. Meg chose
five. Then she chose another. And another.
And another. Now Meg did not have just six
balloons. She did not have just nine. She had
lots and lots and lots!

Meg held those balloons' strings. Then she felt them tug and lift. Meg rose up, up, up.

Meg rode past the gates and past the lake.
"It is getting late," said Meg. "I must take
this gift to Rose. And I can not miss games
and cake."

Then the gulls went past. Peck, peck, pop!
The gulls' bills poked holes in Meg's balloons.
Pop, pop, pop!

At last Meg touched the grass.

"I made it!" said Meg. "I hope I am not late.
I hope I did not miss games and cake."

"You are not late. But is this a new way to
ride?" joked Rose's mother and father.

"It is fun. But next time I will get just five balloons!" Meg grinned.

Make a Greeting Card

You will need:

colored paper

crayons or markers

1. Fold a sheet of paper in half.

2. Write a greeting, such as Happy Birthday, on the front.

3. Draw a picture on the front.

4. Write a note inside the card. You can draw a picture here too. Sign your name.

5. Give the card to your friend!

My New Words

balloon   A **balloon** is a toy made of thin rubber and filled with air or gas.

father*   A **father** is a man who has a child or children.

gas   **Gas** is not solid or liquid and can not be seen. **Gas** that makes balloons rise is called *helium*.

gull   A **gull** is a bird that lives near lakes and oceans.

mother* A **mother** is a woman who has a child or children.

pose To **pose** is to hold your body in one position.

remember* When you **remember** something, you keep it in your mind.

throne A **throne** is a chair on which kings or queens sit.

touch* When you **touch** something, you feel it.

*tested high-frequency words

127

Acknowledgments

Illustrations

5, 16–23 Adam Gustavson; **5–10** Kim Behm; **26, 36–45** Barbara Fiore; **27–30** Brent Hale; **46** Mary Anne Lloyd; **48, 64–69** Michael Rex; **49–57** Pamela Johnson; **70** Beatriz Helena–Ramos; **72–73, 88–95** Robert W. Alley; **96–98** Lynne Avril-Cravath; **97** Philomena O'Neill; **102–108, 127** Ted Dawson; **110–115** Gideon Kendall; **116–126** Jeff Ebbeler

Photographs

Every effort has been made to secure permission and provide appropriate credit for photographic material. The publisher deeply regrets any omission and pledges to correct errors called to its attention in subsequent editions.

Unless otherwise acknowledged, all photographs are the property of Scott Foresman, a division of Pearson Education.

Photo locators denoted as follows: Top (T), Center (C), Bottom (B), Left (L), Right (R), Background (Bkgd).

Opener: (TCR) ©ThinkStock/SuperStock, (CR) ©Jeff Vanuga/Corbis, (C) Stockbyte/Getty Images; **4** ©Spencer Grant/PhotoEdit; **12** ©Michael Pole/Corbis; **13** ©Robert Brenner/PhotoEdit; **14** ©PixFolio/Alamy; **15** ©Spencer Grant/PhotoEdit; **27** ©Olaf Tiedje/Photonica/Getty Images; **32** ©Daniel Mirer/Corbis; **33** ©David Madison/Getty Images; **34** BananaStock/SuperStock; **35** ©Olaf Tiedje/Photonica/Getty Images; **49** Digital Vision; **58** ©Terry Andrewartha/Nature Picture Library; **59** (C) Howard Rice/©DK Images, (C) Getty Images; **60** Digital Vision; **61** (C) Howard Rice/©DK Images, (T) ©Bill Marchel; **62** Stockdisc Premium/Getty Images; **63** (C) Howard Rice/©DK Images, (Inset) ©Jamsen/Jupiter Images; **73** ©Bruce Coleman, Inc./Alamy Images; **74** ©James L. Amos/Corbis; **75** ©Bruce Coleman, Inc./Alamy Images; **76** (TL) ©IT Stock Free/SuperStock, (CR) ©Steve Skjold/Alamy Images; **77** ©ThinkStock/SuperStock; **80** ©Tom Brakefield/Corbis; **81** ©Jeff Vanuga/Corbis; **82** ©Digistock/Alamy; **83** ©Tom Brakefield/Corbis; **84** ©Steve Bloom Images/Alamy Images; **85** ©Danita Delimont/Alamy Images; **86** ©Buddy Mays/Corbis; **87** ©Bryan Lowry /Alamy Images